BE WITH ME LORD
PRAYERS FOR THE SICK

BE WITH ME LORD
PRAYERS FOR THE SICK

Rodney J. De Martini, S.M.

Ave Maria Press
Notre Dame, Indiana 46556

Acknowledgments:

Excerpts from *The Jerusalem Bible*, copyright © 1966 by Darton, Longman & Todd, Ltd. and Doubleday & Company, Inc. Used by permission of the publisher.

Excerpts from the *Good News Bible*, copyright © 1976 by American Bible Society are used with permission, and are indicated *GNB*.

Excerpts from *The New American Bible*, copyright © 1970, by the Confraternity of Christian Doctrine, Washington, D.C., are used by permission of the copyright owner, and are indicated *NAB*. All rights reserved.

_____

Imprimi Potest:
   Very Rev. John F. Bolin, S.M.
   Provincial, Province of the Pacific
   March 16, 1982

Nihil Obstat:
   Maurice F. Shea
   Censor Librorum

Imprimatur:
   Most Rev. Pierre DuMaine
   Bishop of San Jose, California

Library of Congress Catalog Card Number: 82-71881

International Standard Book Number: 0-87793-256-5

© 1982 by Ave Maria Press, Notre Dame, Indiana

All rights reserved.

Photography: John David Arms, 88; Marc R. Francis, frontispiece, 48; Vernon Sigl, 6, 32, 68; Rick Smolan, 12.

Manufactured in the United States of America.

Contents

Introduction

Now Simon's mother-in-law had gone to bed with fever and they told Jesus about her straightaway. He went to her, took her by the hand and helped her up. And the fever left her and she began to wait on them. (Mk 1:30-31)

This gospel scene has special significance for both the sick person and the minister to the sick. Yet Mark's brief and undetailed description leaves us with the question: "How can the healing touch of Jesus be personally experienced by the sick?"

Illness is a common occurrence in the life of every person as it was for this unnamed woman in the gospel. It disrupts our living pattern, often produces feelings of self-pity, helplessness and loneliness, and reminds us that physically we are fragile and mortal. Thus, whether we are pestered by a common cold, hospitalized for a routine operation or faced with the tragic news of terminal cancer, we share a common need. It is a need to replace our fears and frustrations with a sense of confidence and courage. It is a need to experience personally the comfort and peace of being touched by the Lord.

The inevitability of illness certainly does not ensure that we can accept its effects willingly or even find effective ways to show our love and support for those we love who are sick. Too often the reactions of denial and discomfort turn us in upon ourselves to brood or worry aimlessly. The inherent power of our Christian faith to raise our fallen spirit is not called upon. Jesus could have simply visited his friend's mother-in-law and his very presence would have been a caring gesture. Yet he chose to intervene directly and powerfully. Jesus called upon his faith and hers to place this illness in the hands of a loving Father. The power of Jesus' outstretched hand enabled this woman to reach out and serve. This same power and care is the basic inspiration for the prayer forms in this book.

In turning to scripture as a basic component of these prayer units, I believe that we can encounter the most helpful recollections and insights of people who experienced, as we do, the human condition. We need to be reminded that despite our hurts and limitations, especially evident in illness, we have the irrevocable promise of God's personal love and the gift of being saved through the sufferings of Jesus. Our God is not any less familiar with pain and weakness than we are; therefore he understands and, moreover, seeks to share the burden of our hurt and lets us know his personal support.

I have turned to the psalms because of their sensitivity to the whole range of human emotions—anger and thanksgiving, anxiety and peace. Many of the psalms acknowledge the basic enemies of life and candidly remind God that our strength alone is not sufficient to conquer these forces. The psalms call upon God without covering over intense feelings. The psalmist is not afraid to shake his fist at God, knowing that the Lord is not turned away by the honest expressions of his creation. God is not just a fair-weather friend.

Moreover, we should recall that it was the angry cry of Psalm 22 which was placed on the lips of Jesus on the cross. Feeling helpless and alone in the hands of his enemies, Jesus speaks out his feelings of self-pity and hopelessness realizing that only God could understand and care for him in this time of intense need.

It is appropriate to rely upon the expressive words of the psalmist. These cries of real human need can be a springboard of prayer for us. God, who is the source of life, will not turn a deaf ear to his creation in need.

The use of New Testament readings is based upon their value as foundation statements for the Christian life. The many characters and events speak to the human condition and to the persistent attempts of God to minister to his people. The passages were chosen to reiterate familiar incidents in the life of Jesus and the early church, focusing especially on the search for those realities which are permanent and life-giving. Illness so often makes us feel aimless and the quality of our living is disrupted—thus we need to be reaffirmed in the timeless words of the scriptures. In addition, the scriptures can be an antidote to loneliness and introversion. We are reminded in these words that we are part of a larger Christian community extended throughout the ages. We can be led to a sense of commonality with people who, like us, are suffering, but who have turned to the scriptures for comfort and meaning.

The closing prayers are original compositions designed to summarize the scriptural themes. The language is direct, reiterating the personal conviction of the author that feelings of anger, loneliness and frustration can be offered as prayer. Sick people do not need the additional burden of feeling guilty for their feelings or being forced to suppress their complaints to God. Yet every prayer ends with the Easter alleluia as a reminder that death and the forces of fear and weakness have been overcome once and for all in Jesus. God will not turn a deaf ear to our cries; he gave us that promise in his resurrection response to his Son and our brother.

These prayers are primarily intended to be used by a person who is ill. At the same time, those who visit and minister to the sick can find in them an expression of their sentiments which are sometimes too difficult to reveal. Through these expressions of common faith, the patient and the visitor will extend the boundaries of their relationship, no matter how casual or intimate. Together, they can call out to a God who knows and who lived the human condition and redeemed it. There is no better comfort we can give to one another than this reassurance.

I Am Afraid, Lord!

You can turn to the following prayers on those days when you feel especially afraid and powerless in the face of your illness. Your normal routine has been disrupted and you feel cut off from those you love. Your anger and frustration need to be spoken, it hurts too much to keep them bottled up inside! Place yourself—with all your feelings—in the care of your Father, letting him know how weary you feel. You want to be heard and you sense his personal presence to you in your illness. Seek to understand how Jesus dealt with the disappointment of suffering in his own life and try to see this time as one in which you can grow in faith and trust. Let spiritual strength counter the weariness of your body.

1.

Come Save Me, Lord

Jesus reminds us of the healing and uplifting power of faith

"Go back and tell John what you hear and see; the blind see again and the lame walk, lepers are cleansed, and the deaf hear, and the dead are raised to life and the Good News is proclaimed to the poor; and happy is the man who does not lose faith in me." *(Mt 11:4-6)*

Psalm 6
Jesus, Healer of the Sick and Troubled

Lord, don't be angry and rebuke me!
Don't punish me in your anger!
Have pity on me because I am worn out;
    restore me, because I am completely
    exhausted;
    my whole being is deeply troubled.
How long, Lord, will this last?

Come and save me, Lord;
    because you love me,
    rescue me from death.
In the world of the dead you are not
    remembered;
    no one can praise you there!

I am worn out with grief;
    every night my bed is damp from my
    crying,
    my pillow is soaked with tears.

Go away, you evildoers!
    The Lord hears my weeping;
    He listens to my cries for help,
    and answers my prayers.

(GNB)

Responsory

"Everything is possible for anyone who has faith." I do have faith. Help the little faith I have! *(Mk 9:24-25)*

Prayer

Jesus, my Lord and brother, come quickly as the darkness of despair looms over me. Help me to combat this enemy through your life-giving Spirit and enable me to faithfully offer my sufferings in union with your saving passion and death on the cross. May your name be blessed forever!

Amen. Alleluia!

2.

Why Me, Lord?

Those who followed Jesus knew of his compassion for the sick

There was a man named Lazarus who lived in the village of Bethany with the two sisters, Mary and Martha, and he was ill. . . . The sisters sent this message to Jesus, "Lord, the man you love is ill." On receiving the message, Jesus said, "This sickness will end, not in death but in God's glory, and through it the Son of God will be glorified."   *(Jn 11:1, 3-4)*

Psalm 13
The Lord will answer

How much longer will you forget me,
  Yahweh? For ever?
How much longer will you hide your face
  from me?
How much longer must I endure grief in
  my soul,
  and sorrow in my heart
  by day and by night?
How much longer must my enemy have
  the upper hand of me?

Look and answer me, Yahweh my God!

Give my eyes light, or I shall sleep in
  death, and my enemy will say,
  "I have beaten him,"
  and my oppressors have the joy
  of seeing me stumble.
But I, for my part, rely on your love,
  Yahweh; let my heart rejoice in your
  saving help.

Let me sing to Yahweh for the goodness
  he has shown me.

Responsory
"I am the resurrection and the life;
whoever believes in me, though he should
die, will come to life." *(Jn 11:25-26—NAB)*

Prayer

Lord, I am angry and confused, my sickness is beginning to overwhelm me. I want to give so much more in life, Father; so many things I have left undone or unsaid. I humbly ask that you give me the strength to accept my present illness and, if it be your will, that I might regain my health. Forgive my impatience and my unbelief in your constant care for me. I pray in union with Jesus your Son who overcame suffering and death in his glorious resurrection.

Amen. Alleluia!

3.
God Is My Shield

Jesus reminds his followers that suffering patiently borne leads to the joy of resurrection

"If anyone wants to be a follower of mine, let him renounce himself and take up his cross and follow me. For anyone who wants to save his life will lose it; but anyone who loses his life for my sake will find it. What, then, will a man gain if he wins the whole world and ruins his life? Or what has a man to offer in exchange for his life?"   *(Mt 16:24-26)*

Psalm 7
Jesus, my model in the face of despair

Yahweh, my God, I take shelter in you;
  from all who hound me,
  save me,
  rescue me,
or like a lion he will carry me off
  and tear me to pieces
  where no one can save me.

Rise, Yahweh, in anger,
  awake my God!
Confront the raging of my enemies,
  you who demand that justice shall be
  done.

God is the shield that protects me,
  he preserves upright hearts.
God the righteous judge
  is slow to show his anger,
  but he is a God who is always enraged
  by those who refuse to repent.

I give thanks to Yahweh
  for his righteousness,
  I sing praise to the name
  of the Most High.

Responsory
You have given me health and life;
thus is my bitterness transformed into peace.
                    (Is 38:17—NAB)

Prayer

Lord Jesus, I feel weak and helpless in my illness and I want to escape and hide from the possibility of death. Again, I am seeking false comfort for the moment in the denial of death, but I know that this can only lead to anger and despair. Rise up, Lord, and strengthen me now in this time of trial; forgive me for doubting that your grace is always with me. Give me patience with those who seek to comfort me in my illness and courage to face the future. I make this prayer in union with you, Lord Jesus, who accepted sufferings more painful than mine.

Amen. Alleluia!

4.
Be With Me, Lord

Jesus calls us to give example in our lives even when illness drains our strength

"You are the light of the world. A city set on a hill cannot be hidden. Men do not light a lamp and then put it under a bushel basket. They set it on a stand where it gives light to all in the house. In the same way your light must shine before men so that they may see goodness in your acts and give praise to your heavenly Father."

(Mt 5:14-16—NAB)

Psalm 4
Lord, I am afraid

God, guardian of my rights,
    you answer when I call,
    when I am in trouble,
    you come to my relief;
Now be good to me and hear my prayer.

You men, why shut your hearts so long,
    loving delusions, chasing after lies.
Know this,
Yahweh works wonders for those he loves,
Yahweh hears me when I call to him.

Yahweh, you have given more joy to my
    heart than others ever knew.
In peace I lie down, since you alone,
    Yahweh, make me rest secure.

Responsory
"Blest are the sorrowing;
they shall be consoled."   *(Mt 5:4—NAB)*

Prayer

Father, the reality of death touches me
personally in my present illness. It is hard
to remain at peace and accept the fact that
I may soon pass from this life. Yet, I want
to be a sign of hope to others that death is
not the end but an opportunity for more
intimate union with you. Give me the
strength of your grace so that I may
witness to this belief more faithfully and
may always give you thanks and praise for
the persons and events that have entered
my life. I pray this in union with your Son
and my brother, Jesus, who did not give in
to fear or despair in his suffering.

Amen. Alleluia!

5.

I Trust in You, Father

The great apostle, St. Paul, gives us assurance that with faith and hope in the risen Jesus we will achieve a more perfect life

Beloved: flesh and blood cannot inherit the kingdom of God, and the perishable cannot inherit what lasts forever. I will tell you something that has been secret . . . we shall all be changed. This will be instantaneous, in the twinkling of an eye, when the last trumpet sounds . . . because our present perishable nature must put on imperishability and this mortal nature must put on immortality. *(1 Cor 15:50-53)*

Psalm 38

Father, I commend my spirit into your hands

Yahweh, your arrows have pierced deep,
  your hand has pressed down on me.

My guilt is overwhelming me,
  it is too heavy a burden;
my wounds stink and are festering,
  bowed down, bent double, overcome,
I go mourning all the day.

My loins are burnt up with fever,
  there is no soundness in my flesh!
Numbed and crushed and overcome,
  my heart groans, I moan aloud.

Lord, all that I long for is known to you,
  my sighing is no secret from you;
my heart is throbbing,
  my strength deserting me,
  the light of my eyes itself has left me.

My friends and my companions shrink
  from my wounds,
  even the dearest of them
  keep their distance.

But I put my trust in you, Yahweh,
  and leave you to answer for me,
  Lord my God,

now that my fall is upon me,
  there is no relief from my pains.

Yahweh, do not desert me,
  do not stand aside, my God!
Come quickly to my help,
  Lord, my savior!

Responsory

"Anyone who wants to save his life
will lose it.
Anyone who loses his life for my sake
will save it." *(Mk 8:35)*

Prayer

Father, I feel that I am standing on the
threshold between all that has been dear
and familiar to me during this life and a
new and fuller union with you in eternity.
My belief brings me joy and draws me to
proclaim your goodness and mercy. But I
am afraid of making this next step, Lord,
and the pain of my illness overwhelms me
so that I feel abandoned. Come to my aid
with your grace so that in peace I may be
a sign of hope to those I leave behind.
May your name be praised forever and
ever!

Amen. Alleluia!

6.
The Lord Is My Shepherd

Jesus comforts us with the promise of his everlasting faithfulness

"My sheep hear my voice, I know them and they follow me. I give them eternal life, and they shall never perish. No one shall snatch them out of my hand. My Father is greater than all, in what he has given me, and there is no snatching out of his hand. The Father and I are one."

(*Jn* 10:27-30—*NAB*)

Psalm 23
Jesus, I seek your eternal pastures

Yahweh is my shepherd, I lack nothing.
In meadows of green grass he lets me lie.
  To the waters of repose he leads me;
  there he revives my soul.
He guides me by paths of virtue
  for the sake of his name.

Though I pass through a gloomy valley,
  I fear no harm;
  beside me your rod and your staff
  are there, to hearten me.

You prepare a table before me
  under the eyes of my enemies;
You anoint my head with oil,
  my cup brims over.

Ah, how goodness and kindness pursue
  me, every day of my life;
My home, the house of Yahweh,
  as long as I live!

Responsory
"I am the gate.
Anyone who enters through me
will be safe."   *(Jn 10:9)*

Prayer

Lord Jesus, I believe that having passed
through the gate of life in baptism, I will
always have your protection and comfort.
Yet, today, the pains of my illness threaten
to overcome me and cause me to forget all
the good things you have given me in this
life. I pray in confidence that you would
send forth your Spirit to refresh and revive
me as you have always done in the past.
May I continue to witness to your
goodness in this life so that I may be with
you at the heavenly banquet table in eternity.

Amen. Alleluia!

Father, I Seek
Your Forgiveness

Turn to these prayers on those days when your physical illness brings about a sense of guilt for the times you have been selfish or hurtful. Perhaps you find yourself brooding about the missed opportunities you had to act as a Christian, or your spirit is heavy and you even begin to wonder whether your present illness is a result of God's anger. The Lord wants you to unburden yourself of these anxieties. He wants to remind you that he is a compassionate God who never stops loving his children. You need to know that love in a personal way today. Seek him.

7.

The Lord Listens

St. Paul urges us to free ourselves from the burden of sin by submitting to the generous mercy of the Father

You have been taught that when we were baptized in Christ Jesus we were baptized in his death . . . so that as Christ was raised from the dead by the Father's glory, we too might live a new life. . . . That is why you must not let sin reign in your mortal bodies or command your obedience to bodily passions, why you must not let any part of your body turn into an unholy weapon fighting on the side of sin; you should, instead, offer yourselves to God, and consider yourselves dead men brought back to life; you should make every part of your body into a weapon fighting on the side of God; and then sin will no longer dominate your life.

(Rom 6:3-4, 12-14)

Examination of Conscience

1. Have I been allowing self-pity to overcome the sure promise of God's care for me?

2. Have I cooperated with those who are trying to assist me in my illness and sincerely thanked them for their efforts?

3. Have I let anger and frustration silence my thanksgiving for the blessings the Lord has given to me during my life?

4. Have I been a sign of Christian faith and hope to those around me in the humble acceptance of my illness?

5. Have I been persevering in prayer?

6. Do I accept or seek to understand how my sufferings unite me to the death and resurrection of Jesus?

Psalm 116
Thanksgiving to a forgiving God

Alleluia!

I Love! For Yahweh listens to my entreaty;
He bends down to listen to me when I call.
Death's cords were tightening around me,
    distress and anguish gripped me,
    I invoked the name of Yahweh.

Yahweh is righteous and merciful,
    our God is tenderhearted;
Yahweh defends the simple,
    he saved me
    when I was brought to my knees.

Return to your resting place, my soul,
    Yahweh has treated you kindly.
He has rescued my eyes from tears
    and my feet from stumbling.

I have faith, even when I say,
    "I am completely crushed."
In my alarm I declared,
    "No man can be relied on."

What return can I make to Yahweh
    for all his goodness to me?
I will offer you the thanksgiving sacrifice,
    invoking the name of Yahweh.

I will walk in Yahweh's presence
in the land of the living.

Alleluia!

Responsory
"My own peace I give you,
a peace the world cannot give,
this is my gift to you."   *(Jn 14:27)*

Prayer
Father, you are ever faithful and patient
even when I have turned in upon myself
during my illness. I rejoice now because
you have heard the sound of my voice and
offered the life-giving comfort of your
grace. May I strive ever more faithfully to
unite my entire self to your Son who gave
us an example of patient suffering and
may I be an example to others of the
transforming effect of your forgiveness.
All praise and honor to you, source of life
and mercy.

                    Amen. Alleluia!

8.

The Lord Forgives

The call of Jesus never ceases even when we selfishly turn away

"Come to me, all you who labor and are overburdened, and I will give you rest. Shoulder my yoke and learn from me, for I am gentle and humble in heart, and you will find rest for your souls. Yes, my yoke is easy and my burden light."

(Mt 11:28-30)

Psalm 32
Lord, bring me relief from my guilt!

Happy the man whose fault is forgiven,
    whose sin is blotted out;
Happy the man whom Yahweh accuses of
    no guilt,
    whose spirit is incapable of deceit.

All the time I kept silent,
    my bones were wasting away
    with groans, day in, day out;
Day and night your hand lay heavy on me;
    my heart grew parched as stubble
    in summer drought.

At last I admitted to you I had sinned;
    no longer concealing my guilt,
I said, "I will go to Yahweh
    and confess my fault."
    And you have forgiven the wrong I did,
    have pardoned my sin.

That is why each of your servants
    prays to you in time of trouble;
    even if floods come rushing down,
    they will never reach him.
You are a hiding place for me,
    you guard me when in trouble,
    you surround me with
    songs of deliverance.

Many torments await the wicked,
   but grace enfolds the man
   who trusts in Yahweh.
Rejoice in Yahweh,
   exult you virtuous,
   shout for joy, all upright hearts.

Responsory

"If anyone thirsts, let him come to me;
From within him rivers of living water
shall flow."   *(Jn 7:37-38)*

Prayer

Father, I know that you are forever
faithful to those who believe and trust in
you. In my life I have tried to be a worthy
follower of your Son, yet my own
selfishness and weakness have often made
me stray from his example. As I near the
end of this earthly life, I humbly ask your
forgiveness for my sins. Give me strength
of mind and body so that I may continue
to praise you by word and example for all
the blessings you have given me. All glory
be to you, Father, together with your Son
and the Spirit of your love, now and
forever.

Amen. Alleluia!

9.

Take Pity on Me

Jesus encouraged his apostles and all of us who follow him to pray in faith to the Father

Jesus assured his apostles, "Have faith in God. I tell you solemnly, if anyone says to this mountain, 'Get up and throw yourself into the sea,' with no hesitation in his heart but believing that what he says will happen, it will be done for him. I tell you, therefore: everything you ask and pray for, believe that you have it already, and it will be yours. And when you stand in prayer, forgive whatever you have against anybody, so that your Father in heaven may forgive your failings too."

(Mk 11, 22-25)

Psalm 41
Father, grant me peace in your forgiveness

Happy the man who cares for the poor
    and the weak:
    if disaster strikes,
    Yahweh will come to his help.
Yahweh will be his comfort on his bed of
    sickness;
    most carefully you make his bed
    when he is sick.

Yahweh, take pity on me!
    Cure me, for I have sinned against you.

All who hate me whisper to each other
    about me, reckoning I deserve the
    misery I suffer,
"This sickness is fatal that has overtaken
    him, he is down at last,
    he will never get up again."

But Yahweh, take pity on me!
    Raise me up,
By this I shall know
    that I enjoy your favor,
    if my enemy fails to triumph over me.

Responsory
The sting of death is sin.
Let us thank God for giving us victory
through our Lord Jesus Christ.

(1 Cor 15:56-57)

Prayer

Father, I believe that you hear my cries and take pity on the anguish in my heart. Extend your hand as I seek your loving pardon for the selfishness in my life when I placed my own desires and comfort above others' needs and failed to offer you due thanks for your care and mercy. May selfishness, my enemy, be overcome by your grace so that I may never cease to proclaim your praise now and in eternity.

Amen. Alleluia!

10.

Have Mercy on Me

Jesus assures us of the unbounded love of the Father in relating the story of the prodigal son who humbly seeks mercy

Jesus spoke of his return: "While he was still a long way off, his father saw him and was moved with pity. He ran to the boy, clasped him in his arms and kissed him tenderly. Then his son said, 'Father, I have sinned against heaven and against you. I no longer deserve to be called your son.' But the father said to his servants, 'Quick! Bring out the best robe and put it on him; put a ring on his finger and sandals on his feet. Bring the calf we have been fattening, and kill it; we are going to have a feast, a celebration, because this son of mine was dead and has come back to life; he was lost and is found.' "

(Lk 15:20-24)

Psalm 51

Lord, you are good and forgiving

Have mercy on me, O God,
   in your goodness,
   in your great tenderness
   wipe away my faults;
wash me clean of my guilt,
   purify me from my sin.

For I am well aware of my faults,
   I have my sin constantly in mind,
having sinned against none other than
   you, having done what you regard as
   wrong.

Yet, since you love sincerity of heart,
   teach me the secrets of wisdom.
Purify me with hyssop until I am clean;
   wash me until I am whiter than snow.

Instill some joy and gladness into me,
   let the bones you have crushed
   rejoice again.
Hide your face from my sins,
   wipe out all my guilt.

Be my savior again, renew my joy,
   keep my spirit steady and willing;
and I shall teach transgressors
   the way to you,
   and to you the sinners will return.

Save me from death, God my savior,
   and my tongue will acclaim your
   righteousness;
Lord, open my lips,
   and my mouth will speak out
   your praise.

Responsory

"It is only right we should rejoice.
He was dead and has come to life."

(Lk 15:32)

Prayer

Blessed are you, O ever-faithful and patient Father, for you never cease to accept
me in my weakness. In humility, I ask pardon for the times that I failed to respond
as a follower of your Son and placed my
own desires above all else. Yet, while I
have been looking only after myself, you
have never ceased to love and care for me.
May my present illness purge me of
selfishness and allow the inner warmth of
your grace and peace to remind me of my
sonship with you for the rest of my days.

Amen. Alleluia!

I Accept My Sufferings In Union With Jesus

These are times when you want to cast off the sufferings you experience. You wonder why you have to be incapacitated; you have so much to do and so many people who rely on you. You experience the discomfort of being dependent and you sometimes resent the caring hand others are extending to you. Ask the Lord to enable you to understand and to make these words of Jesus your own, "Father, let it be done to me as you will!"

11.
Lord, Hear My Prayer

Our sufferings are not in vain, as the writer of Hebrews reminds us

My son, when the Lord corrects you, do not treat it lightly; but do not get discouraged when he reprimands you. For the Lord trains the ones that he loves and he punishes all those that he acknowledges as his sons. Suffering is part of your training; God is treating you as his sons. . . . We have all had our human fathers who punished us, and we respected them for it; we ought to be even more willing to submit ourselves to our spiritual Father, to be given life. . . . He does it all for our own good, so that we may share his own holiness. Of course, any punishment is most painful at the time, and far from pleasant; but later in those on whom it has been used, it bears fruit in peace and goodness. *(Heb 12:6-7, 9-12)*

Psalm 102
God instructs us in our sufferings

Yahweh, hear my prayer,
  let my cry for help reach you;
Do not hide your face from me when I am
  in trouble; bend down to listen to me,
  when I call, be quick to answer me!

My days are vanishing like smoke,
  my bones smoldering like logs,
  my heart shriveling like scorched grass
  and my appetite has gone;
  whenever I heave a sigh,
  my bones stick through my skin.

He will answer the prayer of the abandoned, he will not scorn their petitions.
Put this on record for the next generation,
  so that a race still to be born
  can praise God:
Yahweh has leaned down from the heights
  of his sanctuary,
  has looked down at earth from heaven,
  to hear the sighing of the captive,
  and to set free those doomed to die.

Responsory

"Unless a grain of wheat falls on the
ground and dies, it remains only a single
grain; but if it dies, it yields a rich
harvest."   *(Jn 12:24)*

Prayer

Almighty God, I struggle daily to understand and accept your ways which are not our ways. While we seek comfort and pleasure in this passing life, you teach us that suffering is the only sure road to eternal life with you. Please help me to bear with my own sufferings more patiently so that I will not be distracted from the call and example of Jesus who, through his suffering, came to reign with you for all eternity.

Amen. Alleluia!

12.

You Are Forever Faithful

Jesus assures us that we are constantly under the care and protection of the Father

"Do not be concerned for your life, what you are to eat, or for your body, what you are to wear. Life is more important than food and the body more than clothing. Consider the ravens: they do not sow, they do not reap, they have neither cellar nor barn—yet God feeds them. How much more important you are than the birds! Which of you by worrying can add a moment to his life-span?"

(Lk 12:22-25—NAB)

Psalm 8
The Father's care is everlasting

Yahweh, our Lord,
    how great is your name
    throughout the earth!

Above the heavens is your majesty
    chanted by the mouths of children,
    babes in arms.
You set your stronghold firm against your
    foes to subdue enemies and rebels.

I look up at your heavens,
    made by your fingers,
    at the moon and stars you set in place—
Ah, what is man that you should spare a
    thought for him,
    the son of man that you should care
    for him?

Yet you have made him little less than a
    God,
you have crowned him with glory
    and splendor,
made him lord over the works of your
    hands,
    set all things under his feet.

Yahweh, our Lord,
    how great is your name
    throughout the earth!

Responsory

"If you, with all your sins, know how to give your children good things, how much more will the heavenly Father give the Holy Spirit to those who ask him."
(Lk 11:13—NAB)

Prayer

Father, sometimes I feel alone in my illness and I am afraid of the future which seems so dark and uncertain. I know that you are always with me, although I must continue to knock down the wall of self-sufficiency which surrounds me. Help me to feel the warmth and see the beauty of your loving presence in creation so that I may always give thanks for your care and receive strength of mind and body to accept the trial of my illness. May your name be blessed today and always, for you are forever faithful.

Amen. Alleluia!

13.

God Raised Him High

St. Paul reminds us that Jesus' great humility led to his suffering and our salvation

His state was divine, yet he did not cling to his equality with God but emptied himself to assume the condition of a slave, and became as men are; and being as all men are, he was humbler yet, even to accepting death, death on a cross. But God raised him high and gave him the name which is above all other names so that all beings in the heavens, on earth and in the underworld, should bend the knee at the name of Jesus and that every tongue should acclaim Jesus Christ as Lord, to the glory of God the Father. *(Phil 2:6-11)*

Psalm 131
Jesus, refuge of the humble

Lord, I have given up my pride,
  and turned from my arrogance.
I am not concerned with great matters,
  or with subjects too difficult for me.
  But I am content and at peace.

As a child lies quietly in its mother's arms,
  so my heart is quiet within me.
Israel, trust in the Lord,
  from now on and forever!

(GNB)

Responsory
"Happy are the poor in spirit,
theirs is the kingdom of heaven." *(Mt 5:3)*

Prayer
Praised be you, O Christ, for your kindness and fidelity and the humble acceptance of suffering for our salvation.
Through the strength of your loving Spirit,
help me to shoulder any infirmities and be
at peace in the knowledge that in union
with your death on the cross I may also
participate in the glories of the resurrection
for all eternity.

Amen. Alleluia!

14.

I Put My Trust in You

*In the face of his own painful suffering
and death, Jesus offers words of consola-
tion*

"To you my friends I say: Do not be
afraid of those who kill the body and after
that can do no more. I will tell you whom
to fear: fear him who, after he has killed,
has the power to cast into hell. . . . I tell
you, if anyone openly declares himself for
me in the presence of men, the Son of
Man will declare himself for him in the
presence of God's angels."   *(Lk 12:4-5, 8)*

Psalm 31
Trust in God as a father

In you, Yahweh, I take shelter;
    never let me be disgraced.
Be a sheltering rock for me,
    a walled fortress to save me!

Take pity on me, Yahweh,
    I am in trouble now.
Grief wastes away my eye, my throat, my
    inmost parts.
For my life is worn out with sorrow,
    my years with sighs;
My strength yields under misery,
    my bones are wasting away.

I put my trust in you Yahweh,
I say, "You are my God."

My days are in your hand,
    rescue me from the hands of my enemies
    and persecutors;
Let your face smile on your servant,
    save me in your love.

Yahweh, how great your goodness,
    reserved for those who fear you,
    bestowed on those who take shelter
    in you, for all mankind to see.

Responsory

God who is mighty has done great things
for me;
his mercy is from age to age on those who
fear him.   *(Lk 1:49-50—NAB)*

Prayer

Father, even while my body is weakening,
may my spirit continue to find its strength
in you. I trust that you will always be
near to me to lead me through whatever
trials bodily sickness may bring. May I
continue to witness to the resurrection
promise of eternal life and thus bring a
sense of faith and hope to those around
me. May your name be blessed today and
always.

Amen. Alleluia!

15.
My God, My God!

*St. Paul encourages us to be unique ex-
amples to all men*

We can boast about our sufferings.
These sufferings bring patience, as we
know, and patience brings perseverance,
and perseverance brings hope, and this
hope is not deceptive, because the love of
God has been poured into our hearts by
the Holy Spirit which has been given us.

(Rom 5:3-6)

Psalm 22
United with the suffering Christ

My God, my God, why have you abandoned me?
I have cried desperately for help,
but it still does not come!

It was you who brought me safely through
birth, and when I was a baby you kept
me safe.
I have relied on you ever since I was born;
since my birth you have been my God.
Do not stay away from me!
Trouble is near,
and there is no one to help me.

My strength is gone, gone like water
spilled on the ground.
All my bones are out of joint; my heart
feels like melted wax inside me.
My throat is as dry as dust, and my
tongue sticks to the roof of my mouth.

Don't stay away from me, Lord!
Hurry and help me, my Savior!

I will tell my people what you have done;
I will praise you in their meeting:
"Praise him you servants of the Lord!
Honor him, you descendents of Jacob;
worship him, you people of Israel!

He does not neglect the poor or ignore
    their suffering;
    he does not keep away from them,
    but answers when they call for help."
                                    (GNB)

Responsory

"If anyone wants to be a follower of mine,
let him renounce himself and take up his
cross and follow me."   *(Mk 8:34)*

Prayer

Lord Jesus, your words on the cross give
me strength and hope. I do not ask to be
relieved of my sufferings but to be helped
to accept them, trusting in the will of the
Father and the hope of securing salvation
for all. Help me to persevere in confidence
when pain brings the darkness of despair
so that I may live in the glory of the resurrection in union with you, your Father and
the Spirit of your love.

                        Amen. Alleluia!

(

16.
My God, Rescue Me

Jesus warns his followers to remain strong

"They will hand you over to be tortured and put to death; and you will be hated by all the nations on account of my name. . . . Many false prophets will arise; they will deceive many, and with the increase of lawlessness, love in most men will grow cold; but the man who stands firm to the end will be saved."

(Mt 24:9-13)

Psalm 71
Growing old in Christ

My God, rescue me from wicked men,
   from the power of cruel and evil men.
Lord, I put my hope in you;
   I have trusted in you since I was young.

My life has been a mystery to many,
   but you are my strong defender.
All day long I praise you
   and proclaim your glory.

You have taught me ever since I was
   young,
and I still tell of your wonderful acts.
Now that I am old and my hair is grey,
   do not abandon me, God!
Be with me while I proclaim your power
   and might to all generations to come.
                                    (GNB)

Responsory
If a man sows in the field of the Spirit
he will get from it a harvest of eternal life.
                              (Gal 6:8)

Prayer

Father, as the span of my life grows shorter, complacency as an enemy leads me to take for granted your goodness in the promise of salvation for your faithful. Through the inspiration of your Spirit help me to continually praise you for the people and events that have entered my life. Help me to stand firm to the end in the face of any difficulties I might encounter in union with the sufferings of your Son, Jesus.

Amen. Alleluia!

I Pray for
Those Who Suffer

You realize today how much your illness turns you in upon yourself—how much your self-pity simply adds to the feelings of depression and powerlessness. You begin to think that you are the only person who experiences so much fear, frustration and inconvenience and this creates a burden of loneliness. You know in your heart that there are others, known and unknown to you, whose sufferings are more burdensome. Reach out to them in prayer and know that you are doing a caring deed from the confinement of your sickbed. Commend them and yourself to the care of a loving God and thus lift your lonely burden from your shoulders.

17.

My Soul Is Thirsting

Paul reminds us that in our baptism we have already died with Christ so that we might live in glory with him forever

Beloved: since you have been brought back to true life with Christ, you must look for the things that are in heaven, where Christ is, sitting at God's right hand. Let your thoughts be on heavenly things, not on the things that are on the earth, because you have died, and now the life you have is hidden with Christ in God. But when Christ is revealed—and he is your life—you too will be revealed in all your glory with him.　　　*(Col 3:1-4)*

Psalm 63
Father, may I be worthy of the kingdom

God, you are my God, I am seeking you,
   my soul is thirsting for you,
   my flesh is longing for you,
   a land parched, weary and waterless.
I long to gaze on you in the sanctuary,
   and to see your power and glory.

Your love is better than life itself,
   my lips will recite your praise,
   my soul will feast more richly,
   on my lips a song of joy
   and, in my mouth, praise.

On my bed I think of you,
   I meditate on you all night long,
   for you have always helped me.
I sing for joy in the shadow of your wings;
   my soul clings to you,
   your right hand supports me.

Responsory
Set your heart on his kingdom first.
Your heavenly Father knows your needs.
(Mt 6:33)

Prayer

Father, mere words cannot express the inner peace which Christian hope in eternal life has brought to me. Yet, I have also felt the fear and uncertainty which weighs upon us in illness when the familiar and comfortable in our lives is taken from our grasp. I pray, now, in hope, that those who have died from illness may have merited your promise of eternal life with the risen Jesus. Give me the strength to continue to bear patiently my sufferings on behalf of those to whom illness has brought despair, so that one day we may praise your name unceasingly in eternity.

Amen. Alleluia!

I Pray for Those God Has Called to Himself

Today your body's weakness is a frightening reminder of how frail your life is. You realize that in spite of all the remedies of medicine, your body will not live forever. You are reminded of friends and loved ones who have gone to the other side of life. They share the fullness of comfort and joy which you seek as well. Place yourself in union with those who know eternal life and the full meaning of Jesus' resurrection. Thus, you can know that the Lord never abandons his loved ones. He cares for us in life and in death.

18.

Age After Age

We pray for the dead with confidence that they have been shown mercy and given everlasting life in union with the Father

One of the synagogue officials came up to Jesus, Jairus by name, and seeing him, fell at his feet and pleaded with him earnestly saying, "My daughter is desperately sick. Do come and lay your hands on her to make her better and save her life." . . . Some people arrived from the house of the synagogue official to say, "Your daughter is dead: why put the Master to any further trouble?" But Jesus overheard this remark of theirs and he said to the official, "Do not be afraid; only have faith." *(Mk 5:22-24, 35-37)*

Psalm 90
Jesus—refuge in life and death

Lord, you have been our refuge age after
   age.
Before the mountains were born,
   before the earth or the world came to
   birth, you were God
   from all eternity and forever.

You can turn man back into dust
   by saying, "Back to what you were,
   you sons of men!"

We too are burnt up by your anger
   and terrified by your fury;
Our days dwindle under your wrath,
   our lives are over in a breath.

Teach us to count how few days we have
   and so gain wisdom of heart.
Let us wake in the morning filled with
   your love
   and sing and be happy all our days.

Responsory
God is God not of the dead, but of the living; for to him all men are in fact alive.
                              (Lk 20:38)

Prayer

Father, your Word among us brings life. Remember those who have died, especially those who have made me a better person by entering my life. As you raised the daughter of Jairus to life, so, too, have mercy on the departed and give me the grace to grow in hope that my own sufferings may bring growth in faith and union with you for eternity.

Amen. Alleluia!

19.

Alleluia Forever!

St. Paul exhorts us to be examples of hope when other men despair in the face of the finality of death

Beloved: We want you to be quite certain about those who have died, to make sure that you do not grieve about them, like the other people who have no hope. We believe that Jesus died and rose again, and that it will be the same for those who have died in Jesus. . . . We shall stay with the Lord forever. With such thoughts as these you should comfort one another. *(1 Thes 4:13-14, 18)*

Psalm 146
The man of hope will sing praise to Yahweh forever

Alleluia!

Praise Yahweh, my soul!
  I mean to praise Yahweh all my life,
  I mean to sing to my God
  as long as I live.

Do not put your trust in men in power,
  or in any mortal man—he cannot save,
he yields his breath and goes back to the
  earth he came from,
  and on that day all his schemes perish.

Happy the man who has the God of Jacob
  to help him,
whose hope is fixed on Yahweh his God,
  maker of heaven and earth.

Yahweh, forever faithful;
Yahweh reigns forever,
  your God, from age to age!

Responsory
Just as all men die in Adam,
so all men will be brought to life in Christ.
(1 Cor 15:22)

Prayer

Lord Jesus, you accepted your death, and with confidence in the Father and love for all people, you proclaimed, "It is finished." May all the good that your servant has done during life merit eternal peace so that he may rejoice in your presence together with the Father and the Spirit of your love. Grant that those of us who remain to carry out your mission of love and life on earth may have the same confidence and peace as we cross over into the eternal kingdom.

Amen. Alleluia!

20.
Praise Is Yours!

As Jesus nears the end of his earthly life he prays for the eternal welfare of his followers

Raising his eyes to heaven, Jesus proclaimed: "Father, I want those you have given me to be with me where I am, so that they may always see the glory you have given me because you loved me before the foundation of the world. Father, Righteous One, the world has not known you, but I have known you, and these have known that you have sent me. I have made your name known to them and will continue to make it known, so that the love with which you loved me may be in them, and so that I may be in them."

(Jn 17:24-26)

Psalm 65
Not an end, but the beginning of eternal life

Praise is rightfully yours, God, in Zion.
Vows to you must be fulfilled,
    for you answer prayer.

All flesh must come to you
    with all its sins;
though our faults overpower us,
    you blot them out.

Happy the man you choose, whom you
    invite to live in your courts.

Your righteousness repays us with
    marvels, God, our Savior;
Your miracles bring shouts of joy to the
    portals of morning and evening!

Responsory
I saw the New Jerusalem coming down
from God out of heaven,
here there will be no more death,
and no more mourning or sadness.

(Rv 21:3-4)

Prayer

Blessed are you, Father, for you lift us out of the finality of this world to experience unending peace and joy in union with you. For those like myself suffering from illness I pray that we may have confidence in your unending care. For those whose illness has brought them to the end of their lives, may they experience your mercy and be found worthy of eternal citizenship in the New Jerusalem.

Amen. Alleluia!

I Thank God
For My Recovery

Today you feel a deep satisfaction and gratitude for restored health. You don't want to forget that the Lord listened to you in the frustrations and fear you voiced in illness, that he sent people to bring comfort to you, and that he nourished you with reassuring words of presence and love. You want to be able to look back at the time of your illness as one in which you grew in trust of God and in the love he manifested through those who cared for you. You want to see this time as one which brought new insight into responsibilities which you can take up anew with energy and faithfulness. You realize that the illness you have borne can make you more understanding of those who enter your life in the future burdened by illness.

21.

I Bless Your Name

We are called to give thanks to the Lord for the good we have received lest we forget that he is the source of all things

Now on the way to Jerusalem he traveled along the border between Samaria and Galilee. As he entered one of the villages, ten lepers came to meet him. They stood some way off and called to him, "Jesus, Master! Take pity on us." When he saw them he said, "Go and show yourselves to the priests." Now as they were going away they were cleansed. Finding himself cured, one of them turned back praising God at the top of his voice and threw himself at the feet of Jesus and thanked him. The man was a Samaritan. This made Jesus say, "Were not all ten made clean? The other nine, where are they? It seems that no one has come back to give praise to God, except this foreigner." And he said to the man, "Stand up and go on your way. Your faith has saved you." *(Lk 17:11-19)*

Psalm 145

The Father has heard my cries for help,
Alleluia

I sing your praises, God my King,
  I bless your name forever and ever.

He, Yahweh, is merciful, tenderhearted,
  slow to anger, very loving and univer-
  sally kind;
Yahweh's tenderness embraces all his
  creatures.

Always true to his promises,
  Yahweh shows love in all he does.
Only stumble, and Yahweh at once supports you,
  if others bow you down,
  he will raise you up.

Righteous in all that he does,
  Yahweh acts only out of love,
  standing close to all who invoke him,
  close to all who invoke Yahweh
  faithfully.

Yahweh's praise be ever in my mouth,
  and let every creature
  bless his holy name forever and ever!

Responsory

"Be compassionate as your Father is compassionate; because the amount you
measure out is the amount you will be
given back."   *(Lk 6:36, 38)*

Prayer

All praise and honor to you, Father, for
the strength of mind and body which has
been restored to me. May this experience
of renewed life lead me to praise your
name more faithfully for the rest of my
days. I humbly ask for the help of your
Spirit, for the light and courage to be a
more faithful follower of Jesus, especially
in being a source of comfort and healing
to others who are in need.

                              Amen. Alleluia!

The Lord Gives Me the Gift of Himself

In your illness, you are especially sensitive to people reaching out to you in love. Most particularly, Jesus extends a loving hand to you today through the Eucharist. He comes to visit you in your sickbed as a friend. He wants to give you strength to combat your weariness. Look to the Lord to hold you in his love because he knows the demands of suffering and the care of a loving Father.

22.

I Give Thanks

In giving the gift of the Eucharist, Jesus bestows on us the promise of life

"I am the bread of life.
He who comes to me will never be
    hungry;
he who believes in me will never thirst.
But, as I have told you,
you can see me and still you do not
    believe.
All that the Father gives me will come to
    me,
and whoever comes to me
I shall not turn him away;
because I have come from heaven,
not to do my own will,
but to do the will of the one who sent me.
Now the will of him who sent me
is that I should lose nothing
of all that he has given to me,
and that I should raise it up on the last
    day.

Yes, it is my Father's will
that whoever sees the Son and believes in
   him
shall have eternal life,
and that I shall raise him up on the last
   day." *(Jn 6:35-40)*

Psalm 111
Thanksgiving for the gift of life

I give thanks to Yahweh with all my heart
   where the virtuous meet
   and the people assemble.

Every work that he does is full of glory
   and majesty, and his righteousness can
   never change.
He provides food for those who fear him;
   he never forgets his covenant.

All that he does is done in faithfulness and
   justice, in all ways his precepts are
   dependable,
   ordained to last forever and ever,
   framed in faithfulness and integrity.

Responsory
"If any man is thirsty, let him come to me!
Let the man come and drink who believes
in me." *(Jn 7:37)*

Prayer

Jesus, you understand our weakness and give us the very source of all goodness and strength in the gift of your body and blood. Just as my body craves food to sustain life, so, too, my spirit is thirsting for you as illness overwhelms me. May this communion, your gift of self, bring joy and comfort to me in the face of pain. All glory and honor to you.

Amen. Alleluia!

The Church Comforts Me

Today you have received the special
ministry of the church through the sacrament of the sick. Open yourself in
thanksgiving to God who has turned this
time of your illness into a source of special
grace for you. Through the prayers and
the anointing which you received, be open
to the assurance of special spiritual
strength in the days ahead.

23.

You Increased My Strength

Paul assures us with the promise of the Lord's assistance that we are never abandoned in the face of sickness and death

When this perishable nature has put on imperishability, and when this mortal nature has put on immortality, then the words of scripture will come true: Death is swallowed up in victory. Death, where is your victory? Death, where is your sting? Now the sting of death is sin, and sin gets its power from the Law. So let us thank God for giving us the victory through our Lord Jesus Christ. Never give in then, my dear brothers, never admit defeat; keep on working at the Lord's work always, knowing that, in the Lord, you cannot be laboring in vain.   *(I Cor 15:54-58)*

Psalm 138
The Father is ever faithful

I thank you, Yahweh, with all my heart,
  because you have heard what I said.
I give thanks to your name for your love
  and faithfulness;
  the day I called for help,
  you heard me
  and you increased my strength.

From far above, Yahweh sees the humble,
  from far away he marks down the
  arrogant.
Though I live surrounded by trouble,
  you keep me alive.
  You stretch your hand out and save me,
  your right hand will do everything for me.

Yahweh, your love is everlasting,
  do not abandon us whom you have made.

Responsory
The prayer of faith will save the sick man,
and the Lord will raise him up again.
                              (Jas 5:15)

Prayer

Lord, I know that you never abandon us
even when we place our needs and sufferings as obstacles to your abiding presence
and care. I thank you for the strength I
have received from the anointing of your
church. May this sacrament give me
renewed strength and the healing power of
your grace so that I may live the re-
mainder of my life in closer union with
you. I pray this in union with your Son
who always showed compassion and
bestowed healing on the sick.

Amen. Alleluia!